Chasing Chariots

Eleven Biblical Lessons For Christian Growth

K. D. Weaver

CSS Publishing Company, Inc., Lima, Ohio

Copyright © 2009 by
CSS Publishing Company, Inc.
Lima, Ohio

Scripture quotations are from Holy Bible, New International Version. Copyright © 1973, 1978, 1984 International Bible Society. Used by permission of Zondervan Bible Publishers. All rights reserved.

Some scripture quotations are from the New Revised Standard Version of the Bible, copyright 1989 by the Division of Christian Education of the National Council of the Churches of Christ in the USA. Used by permission.

Library of Congress Cataloging-in-Publication Data

Weaver, K. D., 1978-
    Chasing chariots : eleven biblical lessons for Christian growth / K. D. Weaver.
        p. cm.
    Includes bibliographical references.
    ISBN 0-7880-2610-0 (perfect bound : alk. paper)
    1. Spiritual formation. I. Title.
    BV4511.W43 2009
    248.4—dc22

                                                                    2008027836

For more information about CSS Publishing Company resources, visit our website at www.csspub.com or email us at csr@csspub.com or call (800) 241-4056.

ISBN-13: 978-0-7880-2610-2
ISBN-10: 0-7880-2610-0   PRINTED IN USA

To my enemies, strangers, friends, and family.

To Reverend Richard Stetler
for giving me the opportunity to lead the garden service.

At Barak's advance, the Lord routed Sisera and all his chariots and army by the sword, and Sisera abandoned his chariot and fled on foot. But Barak pursued the chariots....

— Judges 4:15-16

Table Of Contents

Introduction

Each summer the church where I began my pastoral career did something that was counterintuitive to many churches — it added a service. This summer service was held outside in our garden. The garden service, as we called it, differed from our traditional inside services in formality, and the pastors usually gleaned their messages from the Old Testament.

One summer, I was given the opportunity to design a sermon series for our garden service. As I glanced through Old Testament accounts, one word seemed to consistently appear: chariots. The chariot was a symbol of military power and royal status. Sometimes God would employ this symbol as a sign of divine might for God's people, like when Elijah was taken up to heaven in a fiery chariot, or when God surrounded Elisha and his servant with heavenly chariots for protection against the Aramean army. However, God more often turned this symbol upside down to show how it paled in comparison to who God is and what God can do. The psalmist captured this best when he wrote, "Some trust in chariots and some in horses, but we trust in the name of the Lord our God" (Psalm 20:7). Chariots often function as a sleek-looking shiny obstacle that prevents God's people from being in their divinely ordained places. Naaman would not step down from his chariot to meet Elisha. Elisha's servant, Gehazi, chased after Naaman's chariot out of greed and revenge. The Israelites ran in terror from the Egyptian chariots when they tried to enter the promise land, and once in the promised land the Israelites feared the iron chariots of the Canaanites. Israel rejected God's theocracy and requested a king who would ride in a chariot.

At first glance, the theme for this book is simple — a collection of messages derived from scripture passages that mention chariots. However, after I watched the Holy Spirit work throughout that summer, I realized these sermons were connected by more than merely a reference to a battle instrument, but also spoke to those who desired greater intimacy with God.

This book provides practical approaches to dealing with some of life's challenges that stunt spiritual growth through an insightful look into the Hebrew scriptures. In far too many churches, the Old Testament is viewed as a cumbersome appendage to the holy scriptures. I have met numerous faithful church people who find all the mention of war, bloodshed, and sacrifices as a crude and even inaccurate picture of the God they serve. Contrary to this sentiment, the Hebrew scriptures are filled with an abundance of wisdom and instruction for us. With the exception of one lesson, the teachings in this book are taken from the Old Testament. Each lesson ends with a review of seminal points, questions for reflection as well as a prayer.

May these eleven lessons be a blessing to you so that you can be a blessing to others. May they inspire you so that you can inspire others. May you use them in your daily life so that God may be able to use you more fully.

Deal With Change

As they were walking along and talking together, suddenly a chariot of fire and horses of fire appeared and separated the two of them, and Elijah went up to heaven in a whirlwind.   — 2 Kings 2:11

If we want to identify a frequent cause of our fears, anxieties, or worries, dealing with change would be at the top of the list. Some of the most difficult and painful moments of our lives are intimately linked to the changes we experience. Whether it be a child starting his or her first day of school, two people commencing a new relationship, a couple beginning their journey as parents or grandparents, walking into a new job, visiting a new church, beginning a new living arrangement, ending a professional career, or losing a lifelong mate, friend, parent, or relative, the changes that occur in our lives always create some uneasiness.

Fortunately, we can find some guidance into how to deal with change by looking at the prophet Elisha's experience with change in our passage. Elisha's mentor, teacher, friend, and parent — Elijah — was leaving him; however, Elisha became a benefactor of this change.

Elisha Wants An Inheritance

Elijah told Elisha he was going to leave him, and Elijah asked his student what he would like to occur after his departure. Elisha responded by expressing his desire to be the primary benefactor of his teacher's spiritual qualities. Elisha wanted to benefit in some way from the change that was about to occur.

Elijah told his student that if he wanted to inherit his spiritual qualities, he must see him leave. The teacher did not say Elisha must notice that a change occurred, but must notice the change while it is occurring.

To become a benefactor of change, we must view change as an ongoing process. The people who equate becoming educated to acquiring a diploma, becoming a parent with the birth of a child, death with the cessation of breath, marriage with a particular ceremony, or progress with a job promotion are less likely to benefit from change. The focus in the examples above is on single events or end results. What is missing is that change is always occurring. We are constantly being educated, becoming parents, dying, being born, and moving closer or further away in our relationships as well as growing in our lives. If we were to only look for lessons at set times and places, then we can overlook all the blessings that we can acquire in between our designated markers.

You are wiser and more educated than you were a year ago, but you may not have a diploma to document this fact. Does this mean what you have learned over the last year is less worthy of celebration, reflection, and acknowledgment? You have experienced numerous emotional and spiritual births over the last decade. You have experienced the death of old habits and relationships time and time again. You have experienced a tremendous amount of growth in between your last two job promotions. Begin to notice, acknowledge, celebrate, cherish, and even mourn the process of change in your life, not just the individual results of that process. Elijah told his pupil that if he wanted to benefit from his departure, he must see him leave.

Elisha Gains The Desired Inheritance

A chariot of fire came and swooped up Elijah. Elisha observed the chariot as it moved out of sight. As Elijah continued to ascend into the air the cloak that was on his back fell to the ground. Elisha ran to the spot where the cloak had fallen and picked it up.

A cloak carried two primary functions. The first function was practical — all travelers needed a cloak because it served as both a bag and a blanket. The second function of a cloak was spiritual — cloaks had tassels hanging from the corners. These tassels served as a reminder of the commandments that God had given Israel.

Thus, when Elisha picked up his master's cloak, he picked up something that had both a practical and spiritual use.

To become a benefactor of change, we must gain something from the change that occurs. When a difficult change occurs in our lives, we need to ask ourselves two questions. First, how can this change teach me to be more effective in how I conduct my affairs? Second, what is this change teaching and reminding me about the nature of God? Never allow any change to pass you by without first picking up something practical and spiritual.

Elisha Left Behind Some Of Elijah's Things

Elisha did not only pick up some things, but he also left some things on the ground. When Elijah ascended into heaven, he did not just drop his cloak, but he also dropped his tendency to be intimidated, his fearful spirit, his bitterness and resentment toward the people not doing God's will, and his lack of hope in creation. Elijah dropped some things on the ground that had been detrimental to him as a prophet. Elisha had to make a decision regarding what he would not pick up from his teacher. In order to be a benefactor of change we must leave some things behind. If there are any signs of bitterness, resentment, grudges, hard or hurt feelings within you as a result of a difficult change, the best thing for you to do is leave it on the ground. Be careful of what you take to your next destination.

Elisha Used The Cloak

Elisha did not pick up the cloak and show it off to his friends. He did not tell other people how he obtained Elijah's cloak, nor did he talk about the value of the cloak. Elisha used the cloak to part the waters of the Jordan. In order to be a benefactor of change, we must apply what we have gained from our change.

Prophets At Jericho And The Change

Let us briefly juxtapose how Elisha dealt with the change of Elijah's departure to how the prophets at Jericho dealt with it. The prophets at Jericho verbally acknowledged that Elijah's spirit now rested on Elisha and visibly yielded to Elisha as the new prophetic leader who would serve in place of Elijah. However, notice the contradiction. Even though they verbally acknowledged that Elisha was now the leader and visibly yielded to him, they still wanted to look for Elijah. They appeared to accept change, but they still wanted to bring back the old structure. They desired to try something different, but they essentially wanted to do things the same way.

The prophets of Jericho went to look for Elijah, but he was no longer present on Earth. When we attempt to resurface an old structure, or perhaps the way things used to be, it is like searching for something that essentially does not exist. Thus, we engage in a fruitless exercise. The prophets of Jericho chased after Elijah's chariot, but the chariot was gone.

How we deal with change will determine whether we become a victim or a benefactor of it. Christ continually invites us to experience the benefits of a changed life through him. "If anyone is in Christ, he is a new creation; the old has gone, the new has come" (2 Corinthians 5:17). It is up to us whether we hold on to our old selves or become new creatures through Christ.

Prayer

God, help me to embrace change in a new way. Allow me to be open to the spiritual and practical lessons of change that your Spirit teaches. Guide me so that I will clearly see the gain and easily discard what needs to be left behind. Teach me how to apply all that I have learned. Amen.

Relevant Questions And Sermon Points

How Can We Become Benefactors Of Change?

1. View change as an ongoing process.
2. Gain (learn) something from the change that occurs.
3. Leave some things behind as a result of our experience with change.
4. Apply what we have learned from our experience with change.

Questions For Individual Reflection Or Group Discussion

1. Which of the characters (Elijah, Elisha, or prophets of Jericho) best describes the way you handle change? Why?

2. What was your most vivid recollection of an experience that involved change?

3. How could you have viewed it differently?

4. What did you gain, or could you have gained, from the experience?

5. What was left behind, or should have been left behind, as a result of that experience?

6. What was applied, or could have been applied, to another situation?

7. What insight has God revealed to you through this scripture?

Seek Healing

So Naaman went with his horses and chariots and stopped at the door of Elisha's house.
— 2 Kings 5:9

No matter how successful, prosperous, and happy a person's life may be, there is always at least one thing they would like to change about it. If you have a lot of resources, the relationships in your life are in disarray. If your relationships are great, your resources are limited. If you have a lot of influence and popularity, you have low self-esteem. If you are happy, you are not healthy. If you are healthy, you are not happy. If you thrive in professional settings, you lag behind in social ones. If you have plenty of free time, you are bored out of your mind. If you have fulfilling activities, you do not have enough time. If you have a great marriage, you cannot control your children. If the children are doing great, you and your spouse are on rocky ground.

There is always something. There is always the thorn in the flesh that if we could fix, everything else would be okay. We would be made whole. We would be healed.

Naaman was a person who had it all. He was a successful commander. He was wealthy. He had a loving wife. He had the full support and confidence of the king. He had people waiting and attending to his family. He had the respect of an entire country. Yet Naaman still had one thing he wanted to change about his life: his leprosy. Naaman spent his entire life trying to get rid of the one thing that was interfering with his picture-perfect life — he spent his entire life trying to be made whole.

God Granted Naaman's Success

Being a commander and obtaining all the perks that went along with it was the aspect of Naaman's life that pleased him. His leprosy was the part of his life where he wanted God to be present and change. However, the scriptures tell us that God was already present and assisted Naaman to be a successful commander. Naaman wanted God to do something for him, but he did not realize that God was already doing plenty. Sometimes when we ask God to take care of something, we approach God as if he is not already taking care of the many other things going well in our lives.

There was a son who was doing very well for himself and had recently moved into a new house. One day the son noticed that the sink in his upstairs bathroom was leaking. At first he thought to call a contractor, but then he remembered that his father, who he had immediate access to, was very handy. He called his father and said, "Dad, I have a leaky sink in my upstairs bathroom. Do you think you can come over and fix it for me?"

The father responded, "Sure, son. I will be right there."

The father came to the son's house. The son opened the door and said, "Dad, it's so good to see you. You haven't been over in a while; let me show you some of the updates I have made to the house."

The son took the father to look at the backyard and said, "Dad, I have the greenest grass in the entire neighborhood. I planted a vegetable garden on this side and a flower garden on the other. Everyone always compliments me on my yard."

The son showed the father his deck. "I decided to enclose the deck and create a little green room. And then I placed a patio next to the deck."

The son took the father inside the house. "I put hardwood floors in the kitchen, living room, and dining room. They are made from the finest wood available."

Then the son looked around and said, "I am really glad I was able to scrape the money together to get this place. Dad, as you can see, I have everything else under control. If you can just fix that leaky sink, I will be fine."

The father looked at the son and smiled. "Son, what do you mean you have everything else under control and that you just need me to help with the leaky sink? Who was the one who taught you how to cut the grass?"

"You were, Dad," the son responded.

"Who was the one who taught you how to plant gardens?"

"You were."

"Who was the one who sent the contractors over to your home to build your patio and deck?"

"You were."

"Who was the one who helped you put down those hardwood floors?"

"You were."

"Who was the one who gave you the money for the down payment on this home?"

"You were, Dad."

"So what do you mean that all you need me to do is fix this leaky sink? I am the reason why you even have a sink."

Before you open your mouth and make any request about how you want your life to be, acknowledge all that God has already done. Most of the problems you have reveal the blessings you have received. Having impaired health conditions reveals that you have been blessed with the gift of life. Having a turbulent marriage reveals that you have been blessed with a spouse. Having a difficult, problematic child reveals that you have been blessed with the life of a child. Feeling the pain of losing a loved one reveals that you have been blessed by someone that loved you and impacted your life. Not having a nice home reveals that you have been blessed with having a home. Not having the best parents reveals that you have been blessed by at least having parents. Not having enough resources reveals that you have been blessed by having some resources. The problem is that you have exposed the blessings you have received. Before you ask God for anything, first acknowledge how much God has blessed you. God was the reason for Naaman's success.

A Little Girl Believed

On one of Syria's conquests, a little girl from Israel was captured and assigned to attend to Naaman's wife. This girl was combing the wife's hair one day and she said, "You know that it's too bad what happened to your husband because I know a man who serves a God who can cure him of his condition."

The girl believed that Naaman could be better off than he currently was. Naaman's healing began with a belief that he could be cured. Healing begins to manifest to the surface with some kind of faith that improvement is possible.

Elisha Wants Naaman To Be Clean

Naaman finally located Elisha. He approached the prophet's house in his chariot and waited for the prophet to come to him. Elisha sent out his messenger, who told Naaman to go to the Jordan, wash in it seven times, and he would be cured and cleansed. We must distinguish between being cleansed and being cured. To be cured is to have a physical problem solved. To be cleansed is to be placed back into your proper relationship with God. The Jordan River was considered a sacred river where Yahweh's Spirit and presence manifested itself. Seven was a number of completion and fulfillment. Elisha told Naaman, "Completely surround yourself with God's presence and not only will your leprosy go away, but you will be placed back into a proper relationship with the creator."

There was a mother who wanted to teach her young daughter how to bathe by herself. On the first day, the mother ran some bathwater, went into the girl's room and said, "Alice, go take a bath." The girl went into the bathroom, placed one foot in the bathtub, placed her hands in the tub, splashed some water on her face, dried off, and went to bed. The mother inspected the girl and saw that she had dirt all over her. The next day the mother tried again. She ran some bathwater, went into the girl's room and said, "Alice, go take a bath." The girl went into the bathroom, placed one foot in the bathtub, placed her hands in the tub, splashed some water on her face, dried off, and went to bed. The mother inspected the girl and again saw that she had dirt all over her.

After this continued for a week, the mother became very frustrated and decided to take a different approach. She ran some bathwater, went into the girl's room and said, "Alice, go make yourself clean." The girl asked, "How do I make myself clean?" The mother responded, "First, you must put your body completely into the water. Second, you must use some soap, then you will be clean."

Some of us are washing in the water of God's grace. We are trying. We are making some effort to be clean. We are making some effort to be in a proper relationship with God, but we are missing the soap. We are missing the connection with Christ that we need. Isaiah 1:16 says, "Wash and make yourself clean." 1 John 1:7 says, "The blood of Jesus, his Son, cleanses us from all sin." In order to be healed you must be made clean. In order to be healed you must establish a relationship with Christ, which places you back into a proper relationship with God.

Naaman Was Elevated

Naaman received his command from Elisha. Instead of immediately doing what Elisha said, Naaman allowed his preconceived notions, standards, and knowledge to interfere with taking Elisha's advice. Naaman stood in his chariot. He was elevated over everything and everyone else. He was elevated by his observations of other people being cured. He was elevated by the stories he had heard about how a healing was supposed to happen. He was elevated by his knowledge of the purest rivers in the region. He was elevated by his status and accomplishments. As long as Naaman was elevated in his chariot, was elevated by what he knew and who he was, he would never be able to step down into the Jordan for his healing. In order for you to be healed you must step down from your elevated position. Your knowledge, titles, status, and ego can sometimes be the greatest hindrance to being made whole.

Naaman Becomes Young

Naaman dipped himself in the Jordan seven times and was cured and cleansed. The text tells us that his skin became like that of a young child. Notice Naaman's healing was closely tied to youth. Naaman found out about Elisha from a young girl.

Naaman was convinced to follow Elisha's orders by younger servants (who addressed him as father). Naaman had to become like a little child. He had to let go of his adult experience, knowledge, and ego to receive his healing. "I tell you the truth, unless you change and become like little children, you will never enter the kingdom of heaven" (Matthew 18:3).

In order to be healed, you must become a child. You must be open to the possibility that the world can be radically different from how you know and have experienced it. You must become "naive" enough to believe that Jesus Christ can actually change your life and the lives of everyone you know.

Prayer

Gracious God, we praise you for all the blessings that are unseen and unheard in our daily routines. May we trust that no situation and condition transcends your transforming touch. Teach us how to release pride and hollow knowledge that prevents us from being in deeper relationship with you. Amen.

Relevant Questions And Sermon Points

How Can We Seek Healing?
1. Acknowledge the aspects of your life that are going well.
2. Believe that improvement is possible.
3. Seek to be in a continual and vital relationship with Christ.
4. Step down from what you think you know.

Questions For Individual Reflection Or Group Discussion

1. Make a list of ten things that God has blessed you with this year. How can you make yourself more aware of these blessings on a daily basis?

2. Recount an instance where faith preceded or proceeded a major blessing in your life.

3. Reflect on a situation when you or loved ones were "cleansed," but not "cured."

4. What was a time in your life when "remaining elevated in your chariot" caused you to miss out on God's blessings? Can you think of some instances when "stepping down" (as in humbling yourself) allowed you to become more complete in some way?

5. What are some aspects of your life where "becoming young" could assist you in hearing God's voice?

6. In what ways do you approach your relationship with Christ like an adult, and in what ways do you approach your relationship with Christ like a child?

Sidestep Judgment

So Gehazi hurried after Naaman. When Naaman saw
him running toward him, he got down from the chariot
to meet him. "Is everything all right?" he asked.
                                                   — 2 Kings 5:21

I had a good friend who loved to engage in discussion. We would have conversations about the most mundane things as well as the most perplexing issues. One day we were conversing about a famous athlete who had been arrested. Once he brought up the athlete's name, I rolled my eyes and thought about all the times this person had been in trouble. In a disgusted tone I said to my friend, "That guy has had enough chances. He needs to be locked up for good." My friend simply responded, "Who are you to determine how many chances somebody should get? Who made you the judge over his life?"

There is a tendency within all of us that feels entitled to comment when someone has had enough and when someone has had too much. There is something in our human nature that wants to ensure that the people around us are not too successful and to ensure that people do not get off too easy. There is something inside of us that is comfortable with judging what other people deserve.

If any person was an easy target to be judged, it was Naaman. Naaman was a person who almost had a picture-perfect life. Remember, he was wealthy. He had a loving wife. He was a successful commander. His entire country respected him.

The king loved him. The only thing that was out of place in Naaman's life was his leprosy, and God had just cured and cleansed him. Naaman's healing would be equal to Bill Gates winning the lottery when it is at a record level. Could you imagine if Bill Gates was standing behind you in line waiting to purchase a lottery ticket? Just the fact that he was buying one would seem strange to you.

Naaman's life was so good merely asking for something else would have been strange to most people. When Naaman received his healing many would have said that he received too much. Many would have said, "After all his arrogant ways, his refusal to listen to the prophet's advice and acting like he knew it all, he doesn't deserve to be blessed with anything else. He has had enough chances. He has too much already." It would have been easy for someone to judge Naaman, but Elisha was able to sidestep judgment by keeping a few things in mind.

Elisha Refuses The Gift

Naaman was healed of his leprosy by following Elisha's commands. He returned to Elisha as a believer that Yahweh was the one true God. To show his appreciation, Naaman wanted to give Elisha a gift. This would have been the perfect opportunity to make Naaman suffer for his arrogance and his disobedience. This would have been the perfect opportunity for Elisha to say, "I told you so." This would have been the perfect opportunity for Elisha to determine how much Naaman should pay for all that God had given him in spite of his flaws. However, Elisha refused Naaman's gift.

Elisha was able to sidestep judgment because he understood that God's grace was given freely. "All have sinned and fall short of the glory of the God, and all are justified freely by God's grace through the redemption that came by Jesus Christ" (Romans 3:23-24). It is a lot easier to refrain from judgment once we realize that people are blessed based on God's goodness, not their own.

At first, Naaman wanted to acknowledge God by giving a gift, but when Elisha refused the gift, Naaman decided to acknowledge God by worshiping him each time he made a sacrifice. He acknowledged God by doing something on a continual basis. Elisha understood that God did not want a gift from Naaman — God wanted Naaman's lifestyle.

God does not want you simply to write a big check to the church; God wants you to have a generous spirit. God does not want you simply to go to the soup kitchen; God wants you to become a servant. God does not want you simply to love others; God wants you to embody love to others. God does not want you simply to pray; God wants your speech to become a prayer. God does not want you simply to do one particular thing; God wants to impact the way you do everything. God desires your lifestyle.

Naaman Talks About The King

Before Naaman left with the dirt he requested (to remember and honor the God of Israel), he told Elisha about his relationship to the king. Naaman said, "Elisha, my king is a very feeble man. I escort him to various places and I help him get around. When I take the king to the temple of his god and he bows in this temple, he leans on my arm for support which causes me to bow with him. Could you please forgive me for this?" Naaman told Elisha how the king's feebleness caused him to do something against God's will.

Elisha was able to sidestep judgment because he realized that some of Naaman's errors were the result of the people to whom he was connected. It is a lot easier to refrain from judgment when we realize that many of the inadequacies of people are the results of their connection to others' weaknesses and faults. Once you realize that the young person who stole your car has been bounced around in foster homes where no one ever loved or cared for him, sidestepping judgment becomes a lot easier. Once you realize that the person whose face is scattered all over the news for sexual assault was molested as a child, sidestepping judgment becomes a lot easier.

Once you realize that the person with destructive behavior was physically abused and bullied throughout his life, sidestepping judgment becomes a lot easier. Once you realize that the arrogant person at work with a smart mouth has low self-esteem and has contemplated suicide, sidestepping judgment becomes a lot easier. Once you realize that some of the inadequacies of people are the result of their connection to others' weaknesses and faults, sidestepping judgment becomes a lot easier. This does not excuse anyone's actions. This does not make anyone's actions less wrong, but we must acknowledge that sin is a lot more complex than one individual doing something wrong.

Naaman Is Forgiven

Lastly, Elisha was able to sidestep judgment because he realized that Naaman was forgiven for the sins he committed. 1 John 2:12 tell us, "Your sins have been forgiven on account of Jesus' name." We can sidestep judgment by remembering that others' trespasses, both past and present, are already forgiven through Jesus Christ. If Jesus, who was without sin, could forgive all those who crucified him, then why do we have difficulty forgiving others? "Forgive as the Lord forgave you" (Colossians 3:13).

When we realize that 1) God's grace is free, 2) some people's mistakes are connected to the weaknesses of others, and 3) all are forgiven through Christ, we will have an easier time suppressing the tendency within us to judge others.

Let us compare Elisha's approach toward Naaman with Gehazi's approach. After Naaman headed back home, Elisha's servant determined that Naaman got off the hook too easy. Gehazi decided to make Naaman pay for all the blessings he received.

Time Passed

The first thing that we must note is that a significant amount of time elapses. Naaman had been traveling for a short time period, but even after some time had passed Gehazi still could not stop thinking about Naaman. Gehazi said to himself, "He thinks he has it all. Living in that big house, driving that Mercedes Benz chariot, going home to that beautiful wife, with all his friends and family in perfect health. I can't stand him." Gehazi became consumed with Naaman's life and blessings. Whenever someone makes you upset just by thinking about him or her that is when it is time to step back and relax. No matter what it is, it is not worth your mental anguish.

Determined What Should Be

Once Gehazi finished thinking about Naaman's fate, he determined that Naaman did not suffer enough and he would correct that injustice. Nobody needs someone else to humble him or her.

26

No matter how arrogant, obnoxious, or excessively privileged you think a person is, he or she does not need you to humble him or her. Getting up and attempting to make it through the day is humbling enough. No matter how someone appears outwardly, they have been humbled and will be humbled simply by living life.

Used Guise Of Elisha
When Gehazi reached Naaman he told him he needed some things for Elisha and the school of prophets. Gehazi used the guise of a worthy cause to humble Naaman. Oftentimes, when we judge people and seek revenge we convince ourselves that it is for some greater good. We humble others to "teach them a lesson," "because God would want them to be humble," or "make things right." Too often, just like Gehazi, we use the guise of righteousness and God to justify hurting another person.

Judgment Results In Separation From God
The end result of Gehazi judging Naaman and trying to make him pay was separation from God. Gehazi was the head servant of the prophet Elisha. He was most likely the next in line to lead the community of prophets after Elisha's death. Gehazi wasted his whole career, his relationship with Elisha, and his relationship with God as a result of being consumed by a spirit of judgment.

Any time and energy spent judging someone else and trying to make him or her pay is time and energy that could be devoted to doing God's will. Do not allow what other people do or don't do to distract you from what God has called you to do. Sidestep judgment and continue walking on the path that God has laid out for you.

Prayer
Dear Lord, you forgave us so that we may share your love with the world. Where the spirit of judgment resides in us, subdue it. Where the seeds of compassion and acceptance reside, grow it. Lead us to thoughts, words, and actions that strengthen the body of Christ. Amen.

Relevant Questions And Sermon Points

How Do We Sidestep Judgment?

1. Remember, people are blessed based on God's free grace, not their own worth.
2. Remember that many of people's inadequacies are due to their connection to others' weaknesses.
3. Remember that forgiveness through Jesus Christ is available to all.

Questions For Individual Reflection Or Group Discussion

1. Think about some ways that you display the "no cost" nature of God's grace through your actions toward others. What are some acts that you could take to relay that message more clearly?

2. Can you remember when you have been a benefactor of God's grace? How did that make you feel? How did others perceive your blessings?

3. Can you think of times when a limitation or weakness that you possessed affected someone else? When has a limitation or weakness of another affected you?

4. How does resentment toward others sidetrack you?

5. What image most accurately expresses forgiveness for you? Why?

Execute Your Exodus

When the king of Egypt was told that the people had fled, Pharaoh and his officials changed their minds about them and said, "What have we done? We have let the Israelites go and have lost their services!" So he had his chariot made ready and took his army with him.
— Exodus 14:5-6

All of us have aspects of our lives that we need to separate from and leave behind. Some of us have bad habits, while some of us have emotional, spiritual, and physical states that we need to separate from and leave behind. Some of us have relationships that we need to separate from and leave behind. Some of us have mentalities and thought patterns that we need to separate from and leave behind. Some of us have roles that we need to separate from and leave behind. Some of us have environments that we need to separate from and leave behind. Some of us have recurring circumstances and situations that we need to separate from and leave behind. There is no better place to search for revelation into leaving behind detrimental aspects of our lives than the account of the Israelites' exodus from Egypt.

The Israelites were the lowest class of people in Egypt. They were used and abused by the Egyptian authorities. They were prevented from moving upward in Egyptian society. They lived in slums. Their male children were ordered to be killed. God said, "Enough is enough; it is time for my people to leave Egypt and never return again."

Egypt Used To Be Pleasant

Egypt was not always an unpleasant place for the Israelites to dwell. Remember Joseph? He was second in charge of Egypt. He saved the Egyptians and surrounding region from starvation. Then he brought his family and his people into the land of Egypt and they lived there and prospered. After some time had passed, Egypt evolved into a hostile environment and it was time for the Israelites to go.

The reason why some of us have difficulty even desiring to leave detrimental places in our lives is because we remain focused on how pleasant the situation used to be. Some of us are being blocked from seeing the negative repercussion of some habits, relationships, mentalities, roles, environments, circumstances, and situations because we have held on to memories of when those aspects of our lives were good. Egypt used to be a great place to reside, but it was time for the Israelites to go.

Israelites Go To The Sea

As the Israelites exited Egypt, God told them to go to a particular location near the sea. This location was directly opposite Baal Zephon. Baal Zephon was a city dedicated to the god, Baal, who symbolized a culture and a way of life opposed to Yahweh. Then God told Moses, "Once the Israelites are located in this position Pharaoh and the Egyptians will think they are lost." The Israelites could have left Egypt another way, but because they were following the voice of God they ended up by the sea, which seemed like a strange exit route to everyone observing the situation.

When we try to separate and leave behind an aspect of our lives that is detrimental, we should do so in a way that displays the distinctiveness of our faith. When we do that it will seem strange to others. It may seem strange why we still pray for someone when ending a relationship with him or her. It may seem strange why we would be concerned about an environment that we just left. It may seem strange why we'd want to assist others who possessed the same detrimental tendencies that we once possessed, but the way we separate and leave behind an aspect of our lives should show the distinctiveness of our faith.

Pharaoh's Power Displayed

Pharaoh realized that the Israelites left and regretted letting them go. He prepared his chariots and 600 additional chariots to chase after them. The Israelites thought everything was going well and suddenly they saw the Egyptians steadily approaching. The Israelites knew that it was only a matter of time before the Egyptians, who were in chariots, would catch up with them, who were on foot, and they became scared. At that moment, they had to decide whether they were going to believe in the power of Pharaoh's chariots or the Lord.

Psalm 20:7 tells us, "Some trust in chariots and some in horses, but we trust in the name of the Lord our God." When you execute your exodus, you must believe that God's power trumps any other force present on earth.

God Stands In Between

Once the Egyptians began to catch up with the Israelites, God's presence moved from in front of the Israelites to behind them, which created a buffer between the Egyptians and the Israelites.

In my neighborhood, there is a big dog that often breaks loose from his chain and roams around. One day when I came home and got out of my car, I saw this dog on the other side of the street. Further up that same side of the street was a young boy who had just left school. As the boy proceeded up the street he noticed the dog and the dog noticed him. At that point, the boy made a tragic mistake — he began to run. As soon as the boy started running, the dog started running after him.

Even though there was a significant distance between the boy and the dog, the four-legged animal quickly made up the difference. Just before the dog was about to catch the boy, the boy jumped over a fence. The boy hit the ground hard and was obviously disturbed because he could still see the dog through the fence and hear it growling. After a few moments passed, the boy realized that even though the dog was barking extremely loud and looked very intimidating, the dog could not touch him while he was behind the fence. The boy started dancing and swinging his book bag in the air because he now had a newfound confidence behind the fence.

When you place yourself on the right side of God's fence, something that wants to get to you is going to have to go through God. The reason why David was confident when he fought Goliath, the reason Jacob could endure the deceitfulness of Laban, the reason Gideon's smaller army could boldly attack a larger army, and the reason Samson did not fear the Philistines was because they believed that there was a fence of protection in between them and those who were against them.

Path Took Some Time

Moses stretched out his hand and the wind started to blow. Some of the Israelites looked at the Egyptians charging and wanted to go, but Moses said, "No, not yet." Then the part in the sea went deeper and deeper. "Can we go now?" "No, not yet." Then the part in the sea exposed the bottom of the sea. "Can we go now?" "No, not yet." The part began to expose more and more of the bottom of the sea. "Now?" "No." Finally, the exposed bottom slowly started to become dryer and dryer and the Israelites walked across. God made a path where there was no path, but the path did not come about instantly.

To execute our exodus, we must exert some patience while God is making a way for us. God did not deliver Noah and his family instantly from the flood. They stayed on a boat for some time. Abraham and Sarah did not receive their promised child right away. They had to trust God a little longer. Joseph did not receive the fulfillment of his dreams when he first had them. He had to dwell in a pit and a prison. Joshua did not receive the promised land immediately. He had to walk around Jericho seven times first. Mary did not understand how her son would be the Messiah. She had to watch him grow up. We must allow some time for God to make a way for us.

Chariots Fall Apart

One of the most powerful instruments in the ancient world fell apart when it was used against God's people. No matter how gigantic, strong, or potentially destructive a person, place, or circumstance can be to your life, it has no power when you operate in

God's will. Isaiah 54:17 tells us, "No weapon forged against you will prevail, and you will refute every tongue that accuses you. This is the heritage of the servants of the Lord."

Notice the Israelites' exodus from Egypt was dependent upon one crucial thing: God's prompting. When they left and how they left started with God. As a people of faith, we must constantly make ourselves attentive to God's voice through prayer, meditation, fasting, and scriptures. Through these spiritual disciplines and others, we will be able to identify our own personal "Egypts" and the best way to exit from them.

Prayer

Almighty God, you provide a safe haven from our enemies, yet your faithfulness is sometimes overshadowed by our fears. We cling to the past because the future appears uncertain. Strengthen us to move with confidence in your path. May your Spirit focus us. Divert our attention from all that can harm us and direct it toward your saving grace. Amen.

Relevant Questions And Sermon Points

How Do We Execute Our Exodus?
1. Do not become sentimental about a detrimental place.
2. Separate in a way that shows Christian distinctiveness.
3. Believe that God's power is greater than any power against you.
4. Understand that deliverance takes time.

Questions For Individual Reflection Or Group Discussion

1. List a few aspects of your life that were once pleasant but are no longer. When did you realize the change? Why do you believe this change occurred?

2. What are some of the difficult parts of separating from something detrimental in your life? Does being Christian complicate how you leave something behind? Why or why not?

3. How is your relationship with God strengthened or hindered during a time when you are attempting to separate and leave behind a negative aspect in your life?

4. What are some essential skills or attributes that you need to pull away from detrimental aspects affecting your life? How do you develop these attributes if they are lacking?

Make Proper Requests

This is what the king who will reign over you will do:
He will take your sons and make them serve with his
chariots and horses, and they will run in front of his
chariots.   — 1 Samuel 8:11

Samuel led the Israelites throughout his entire adult life. As he grew older, he began to mentor his two sons to succeed him just as Eli had mentored him. Once Samuel's two sons began to judge and interact with the people, the Israelites realized that Samuel's sons were not as faithful and honest as their father. The succession process from one Israelite judge to another was off to a problematic start. The elders of Israel got together, went to Samuel and said, "Samuel, we all know that you are not getting around as fast, you are forgetting things, moving a little slower, your eyesight is not as sharp, your hearing is not as good, and you won't be with us that much longer. And your sons, no offense meant, don't need to be praying for anybody else because they need to be prayed for right now. This succession process of the judges is not working; we think having a king would be so much easier. Just give us a king, Samuel. Let's forget about this whole succession process."

Detrimental Elements In Request
The elders' request possessed two detrimental elements. First, the request was premature. Samuel was not dead yet. They still had an honest, righteous leader present with them who lived long enough to see the reign of not one, but two kings.

Sometimes we are so worried about what is going to happen next week that we can't see that today is a good day. Today, everything is working fine. Today, you are able to get out of bed. Today, you can see somebody you love. Today, you are able to walk and talk. You do not know what tomorrow is going to bring, but right now you are okay. "Who of you by worrying can add a single hour to his life?" (Matthew 6:27).

The second detrimental element this request contained was frustration. Their frustration about the actions of Samuel's sons led them to seek an alternative to God's system. Being guided by impatience and frustration will ultimately lead to a departure from God's ways.

When frustration and impatience consume us, these are the moments when we are most tempted to stop loving and start resenting and judging others. These are the moments when we stop seeking to be last and start pushing to be first. These are the moments when we stop forgiving and start seeking revenge. These are the moments when we cease from using uplifting language and begin to verbally tear people down. These are the moments when we refuse to share and start to hoard. These are the moments when we refuse to listen and only desire to be heard. When frustration and impatience abound, these are the moments when we depart from God's ways and seek alternatives in the world around us. Frustration and impatience are two of the primary reasons why many God-fearing people make some ungodly decisions and requests.

God said, "Samuel, don't take personal offense to their request because it shows their disregard for me, not you." The requests that we make imply some type of commentary on God's providence. Many times requests to God translate into a statement like, "God, even though you are all-knowing, all-powerful, and omnipresent, obviously you have forgotten a few things. Let me tell you what I need and should have."

Warning About The King

God said, "Samuel, give them what they want but warn them about the repercussions of their desires." In verses 10 through 18, Samuel tells the people that three things will happen as a result of their request for a king. First, the king will take three things from them: their sons, their daughters, and their fields and livestock. Sons were valued because they continued the family lineage.

Daughters were valued because of their physical labor in running the household. Fields and livestock reflected a person's possessions and wealth. Samuel told the Israelites that what you desire is going to take your legacy, your physical strength, and your wealth. What we desire and pursue in the present will shape how people remember us when we are gone. While we are here, our physical energy and resources will be depleted by our pursuits and desires.

Second, a king will make Israel serve him. Samuel warned the people that what they desire will become their master. They will have to revolve around and conform to their desires.

Last, Samuel told the people that they will eventually want a respite from the king that they have requested. The things that you desire now are going to be the very same things that you seek relief from later. You desired a spouse and you got one, but now you understand the importance of alone time. You desired some children and grandchildren and you got some, but now you know the importance of multiple babysitters. You desired a big house and you got it, but now you are grappling with the magnitude of a thirty-year bill. You desired to have the latest technology and vehicle, but now you know the high maintenance that it requires. You desired the top job, but now you have the weight of the responsibilities that come with it. What you desire now, you will seek relief from later.

Sometimes, the worst thing that could possibly happen is for us to receive what we want, when we want it. Israel received what she wanted, when she wanted it. Just three kings later they were being oppressed by the king that they desired. As a result of Israel not making the proper request, her request came back to haunt her.

Proper Requests

How do we make requests so that they do not come back to torment us?

In order to make a proper request first, we must acknowledge we do not know what is best for us. "... the Spirit helps us in our weakness. We do not know what we ought to pray for, but the Spirit himself intercedes for us with groans that words cannot express" (Romans 8:26). "Your Father knows what you need before you ask him" (Matthew 6:8).

You must be at a high level of spiritual maturity just to know what to ask God for. All of us, at least sometimes, need to seek discernment about what we should pursue and desire. We must not seek after what we want but what God would want for us, which is better than we could ever want for ourselves. This is why it is so important to always practice Christian meditation. You must allot time when your spirit can be completely attentive to God.

Second, after being open to God's will, we must ground ourselves in it. We must get to a point in as many aspects of our lives as possible where what God desires is the same as what we genuinely desire.

Third, we must make our requests based on God's will. "This then is how you should pray: Our Father in heaven, hallowed be your name. Your kingdom come. Your will be done, on earth as it is in heaven" (Matthew 6:9-10).

Once we ground our petitions in God's desires for us, there is nothing we will be denied. "The desires of the righteous end only in good" (Proverbs 11:23). Why do they always end in good? The righteous desires always end in good not because of who the righteous are, but because of what the righteous have come to desire. "This is the confidence we have in approaching God: that if we ask anything according to his will, he hears us. And if we know that he hears us — whatever we ask — we know that we have [it] ..." (1 John 5:14-15). Never forget that making the proper request is essential to our spiritual maturity.

Prayer

Precious Lord, we often make decisions based on our own ways and understanding, but our ways and understanding are not as honorable and worthy as yours. Create clean hearts in us. Let our actions reflect the desire for your kingdom to come and your will to be done. We surrender to you this day. Amen.

Relevant Questions And Sermon Points

How Can We Make The Proper Requests?
1. Acknowledge that you do not know what is best for you.
2. Seek God's will.
3. Become aligned with God's will.
4. Make petitions based on God's will.

Questions For Individual Reflection Or Group Discussion

1. What memorable request have you made that resembles the Israelites' request?

2. What did you learn in hindsight that you did not know when the request was made?

3. How could you have sought and aligned yourself with God's will in that situation?

4. What steps can you take to explicitly include God in your requests in the future?

Seize What God Has For You

At Barak's advance, the Lord routed Sisera and all his chariots and army by the sword, and Sisera abandoned his chariot and fled on foot. But Barak pursued the chariots....   — Judges 4:15-16

How can the book of Judges speak to us? How can this book that contains accounts of bloodshed, war, strange names, and customs from a distant time say anything relevant to us? As Christians, we believe that studying the Bible is a spiritual activity. By the grace of God and our faith, we are able to go through the text and have insights revealed to us as people of faith, as a particular congregation and as individuals. Without our faith and our relationship with Christ, we get stuck in the text. All we can see are the strange names, customs, the bloodshed, and the war. With our faith and relationship with Christ, a completely new layer of God's insight for us is revealed. This is the insight that we identify as the word of God. Now, with our eyes of faith and by God's grace, we explore what the book of Judges has to say in reference to seizing what God has for us.

Deborah Sends For Barak

In this chapter of Judges, we find that the Israelites are being oppressed by the Canaanites. The commander of the Canaanite army was Sisera. He reportedly had 900 iron chariots that he used to persecute Israel. During this time, Deborah was the moral, legal, and political leader of Israel. Deborah sent someone to retrieve Barak. Barak came to her and she told him to take 10,000 soldiers from his hometown and the surrounding area to Mount Tabor and wait to attack Sisera's army.

Barak did not receive this assignment by accident. He was not simply near Deborah and she said, "Hey, you, why don't you get some soldiers and head over to this mountain?" Deborah sat back in her chair and thought about all the possible people available for this assignment. Her close friends and associates gave her suggestions. She considered Jonathan, Joshua, Sarah, Michael, Rachel, and Samuel. "No, no none of them will work. Get me Barak." Deborah sent for Barak.

As a child, I always rushed to finish my homework because after I completed it, my mother would send me outside. I was acutely aware that once out the house I only had a set amount of time. First, I would make sure that I could see all my friends. Then I would go to the park. I would also make sure that I was able to play my favorite games. By the time I saw the people that I wanted to see, went to the places I wanted to go, and played the games I wanted to play, I knew that my mother would be sending someone to get me to come back in the house.

Before you were even conceived, God identified something about your spirit that was needed here in this physical life. Now that you have come into this world, God is sending you out to meet particular people, to visit some particular places, and to engage in some particular things. After this is over, God will send for you to come back to him. In John 20:21, Jesus said, "Peace be with you! As the Father has sent me, I am sending you." God sent you to this world, God sends you in this world, and God will send for you from this world one day. You have been specifically chosen and sent to seize some particular things in this lifetime.

Barak Wants Deborah To Come

Deborah continues, "God does not just want you to go into battle, but God assures me that you will be victorious." After Barak heard about his assignment and how the victory was ensured, he responded, "I will do it, but only if you, Deborah, go with me."

Barak wanted some extra assurance and security that God was going to do what he said he was going to do. "Not one word has failed of all the good promises he gave ..." (1 Kings 8:56). What God has for you has already been guaranteed. It does not matter

42

how many people are supporting you, how many people like you, or what you have because what God has for you has already been ensured.

God's Uses Israel's Enemies To Teach Her

Review Judges 2:21 — 3:2. The generations of people that remembered leaving Egypt, receiving the laws from Mount Sinai, and conquering and obtaining the promised land had died. Now Israel was made up of a new generation that never had to fight and struggle for their land, nor had to depend on God to obtain their land. So God said, "I am going to keep the enemies of Israel around to teach them how to fight and how to depend on me and my law."

In other words, Barak was not sent into battle simply to defeat Sisera and the Canaanite army, but he was sent to learn how to fight and trust in the Lord. The process that God takes you through in accomplishing something is just as important as what you accomplish. God doesn't just have certain things for you, but he also has lessons for you to learn while seizing these things. Barak was so focused on the outcome of the battle that he never considered that the act of going to battle itself was part of what God had for him.

Deborah Reminds Barak

Deborah agreed to go with Barak. Barak gathered up his soldiers, went to Mount Tabor, and waited for Sisera's army. Sisera's army came into Barak's sight and Deborah reminded him that the Lord had already ensured his victory and encouraged him to attack. Deborah did not fight for Barak, but she reassured him of what he already knew.

Barak Pursues An Empty Chariot

Barak fought against Sisera's army and started to defeat them. Sisera realized that he would soon lose this battle so he left his chariot and fled by foot. However, Barak continued to pursue after Sisera's chariot. He assumed that the commander who he needed to capture was in the chariot.

What God has for you is not always in the elevated places. Luke 9:48 says, "For he who is least among you all — he is the greatest." Matthew 19:30 tells us, "Many who are last will be first." God has some things for you to seize that are in places that lack praise, that lack reward, that are not desirable, that lack significance and prestige, and that will place you at the very bottom. But if you are able to seize these things, you will be able to unlock a form of greatness foreign to most of the world. Because Barak chased the empty chariot, he was not able to complete the victory that God intended for him.

In order to seize what God has for you, remember: You were sent to obtain it, you are guaranteed to have it, there are some lessons to be learned in the process of gaining it, and what God has for you is not always in elevated places.

Prayer

Loving provider, from you all our blessings flow. This world tells us to lie, cheat, and compete to get want we want; you tell us that you have set aside a place just for us. This world operates based on divisions and hierarchies, but your bounty is great enough to be extended to all. Give us the courage to pursue all that you have placed before us in a spirit of love and integrity. May we become the people of God that you created us to be. Amen.

Relevant Questions And Sermon Points

How Can We Seize What God Has For Us?
1. Live as if you were selected and sent to obtain some specific things.
2. Remember that the process of obtaining what God has for you is just as important as the goal itself.
3. Look for what God has for you in places and situations that are not elevated and desirable.

Questions For Individual Reflection Or Group Discussion

1. How can you attempt to discern what God has sent you to this earth to do? Do you have any beliefs or feelings about what God has sent you to do?

2. What ways do you try to "secure" your destiny for what you believe God has for you or what you simply want for yourselves?

3. Think about some professional, personal, academic, spiritual, social, or other goals that you have tried to accomplish. What lessons did you learn in the pursuit of those goals? Did you recognize God's hand in your quest for those things?

4. What are some instances in your life where you need to be reminded of God's goodness? Why?

5. Think about some times when you have pursued something that you thought God wanted for you, but realized that it was really elsewhere. What were some factors that led you in the non-God-ordained direction?

Outgrow Your Blessings

*You are numerous and very powerful. You will have not
only one allotment but the forested hill country as well.
Clear it, and its farthest limits will be yours; though
the Canaanites have iron chariots and though they are
strong, you can drive them out.* — Joshua 17:17-18

If we were to think of the words most frequently affiliated with God, the word "promise" would be near the top of the list. One of God's most definitive acts was an extension of a promise to Abraham that his offspring would receive a new land.

Abraham carried this promise with him throughout his life, and before he died, he reminded Isaac that there was this God who had made a promise. Isaac took this promise and carried it with him throughout his life, and before he died, he reminded his son, Jacob, that there was this God who had made a promise. Jacob carried this promise with him throughout his entire life, and before he died, he reminded Joseph and his brothers that there was this God who had made a promise. Joseph and his brothers carried this promise with them when they lived in Egypt, and before they died they reminded their daughters, sons, granddaughters, grandsons, and even great-grandchildren that there was this God who had made a promise.

When these children, grandchildren, and great-grandchildren were oppressed and enslaved in Egypt, Moses reminded them that there was this God who had made a promise. One of the most consistent identifiers of the God of the Israelites was that he was a God of promise.

The book of Joshua is so monumental because in it we see the promise that God made centuries ago with Abraham manifested. The people of Israel finally received their promised land.

Manassites Received Their Land

Joshua summoned all the tribes of Israel and divided the land amongst them. He told each tribe which particular parts of the promised land they had dominion over. The Manassites along with the rest of Israel had received a blessing that was being formed and shaped before they even existed.

This generation of Israelites was not present when Abraham wandered in a strange land, uncertain if God would ever give him a descendant. They were not there when Sarah experienced the anguish of having a closed womb. They were not there when Isaac was placed on that altar. They were not there when Jacob wrestled with the angel of God and was cheated out of seven years of labor. They were not there when Rachel and Leah feuded. They were not there when Joseph's brothers left him in a dry well to die. They were not there when the Israelites escaped Egypt on foot as they were chased by chariots. They were not there when Israel had to cross the Red Sea. This generation of Israel was not there through all the struggles and hardships that had to be endured to receive the promise, yet this generation received the promised land.

God does not need your presence to bless you. All of us have had some people that came before us who struggled, endured hardships, persevered, and died, and in those acts, our blessings were being shaped and formed. As a result of who and what came before you, you were able to be educated to a greater degree. As a result of who and what came before you, you were able live in a better neighborhood. As a result of who and what came before you, you were able to be more loving and kind. As a result of who and what came before you, you were able to be a better parent. As a result of who and what came before you, you have certain rights and privileges. As a result of who and what came before you, you are able to live a healthier, more balanced life. As a result of what was being formed and shaped before you even existed, you are able to be blessed today.

Manassites Cannot Live In Their Land

The Canaanites lived in the land that Israel had conquered. Joshua had already defeated them and their land had been divided.

When the Manassites went to settle in their portion of the promised land, the Canaanites refused to acknowledge that the region belonged to them. The Manassites had received ownership of this land, but someone was preventing them from claiming it.

One day God decided he was going to buy his people a house. After he thought about it for a while he decided that he did not merely want to buy them a house, but rather a mansion. God went to a mortgage lender. He told the mortgage lender that he wanted to buy a mansion for his people, and then immediately transferred the deed of the mansion to his people so they could have complete ownership of it. After God finished explaining his plan, the mortgage lender told him he could not totally relinquish the deed to the mansion until the loan was paid off. God said, "That is not going to work. I want my people to have complete ownership over this mansion. That is okay. I will save up and pay for the mansion myself." God worked and saved for more than 500 years. After saving and investing in generation after generation, he had finally accumulated enough to buy the mansion for his people. He turned the deed over to them and told them the mansion was completely theirs.

The Manassites had already received their mansion. They completely owned it. They had the deed to it, but something was preventing them from moving into their new home.

Some of us have some long-standing issues that are preventing us from living in the blessings that God has given us. You might have some detrimental attitudes, dysfunctional relationships and family dynamics, health problems, prior commitments, prejudices and preconceived notions, or self-esteem issues that are preventing you from claiming the blessing that God has already purchased for you.

Manassites Take The Land

The Manassites eventually got to a point where they were able to subdue the Canaanites and occupy the land God has given them. Notice that although the Manassites were able to live in their land, the Canaanites were still present.

There are some issues that will be with you for the rest of your life. We are all flawed and broken vessels. Even though you may never be able to completely eliminate some issues, you can still claim what God has for you if you can keep those issues in check. The true nature of your problems are not your detrimental attitudes, dysfunctional relationships, family dynamics, low self-esteem, health problems, prior commitments, or your prejudices or preconceived notions, but allowing these issues to prevent you from living in the blessings that God has for you. God is saying, "I don't want you to be perfect. But I want you to get to the point where your imperfections are not interfering with what I have for you."

The Land Is Not Enough

During the time when the Manassites subdued the Canaanites and gradually moved into their God-given land, they grew in numbers and in strength. They had grown so much while claiming their land that it was no longer sufficient for them.

When I was young, my parents took me to the store to purchase a suit. I tried on a number of different suit jackets. I finally found one suit jacket that I liked, but I noticed that the shoulders of the jacket were broader than my shoulders. When I asked the store attendant what could be done to make the jacket fit better, he told me, "You have to do some push-ups and grow some broader shoulders."

After one year, the jacket that was too big for me fit just right. When another year passed, the jacket that fit me just right was too small for me because I was still growing.

God intentionally gives you something bigger than you think you can handle to see if you will grow into it. Some of you will not only grow into what God has for you, but you will outgrow it. In the process of walking with the Lord and putting your issues in check, you will become stronger and more spiritually mature than you ever were. As a result of this growth and maturity, some of the positions, activities, aspirations, desires, and relationships that were good enough for you at one time will no longer suffice. Matthew 25:21 reads, "Well done, good and faithful servant! You have been faithful with a few things; I will put you in charge of many things. Come and share your master's happiness."

We must distinguish outgrowing our blessings from simply wanting more. When you simply want more it usually starts from viewing something else. You have compared where you are and what you have with where others are and what others have, thus you become dissatisfied. Your dissatisfaction comes from what you have observed. Notice the Manassites did not tell Joshua their land was not enough because they saw another piece of land. When you outgrow your blessing, it is based on how far God has brought you. Your spirit becomes so restless that you feel that your environment or context is no longer adequate for the plan God has for you.

Joshua's Advice

Joshua told the Manassites, "If you have really grown that much, then go out and claim more land." The Manassites told Joshua how far they had come, but Joshua told them how far they could go. Growth is not just an indication of what you have been through, but it is also an indication of what you can do.

Joshua And The Manassites' Conversation

Joshua told the Manassites that they were capable of expanding their territory and simply needed to clear the land. The Manassites responded, "We can't expand because there are Canaanites in the region with iron chariots that will never allow us to live there." Joshua countered, "Don't worry about what will prevent you from living in the expanded territory. Just clear the forest and the land will be yours. Don't worry about the iron chariots of the Canaanites because before you can live in the region you are going to have to cut down the trees on the land first."

What is a primary human use for trees? Trees serve as a source for shade. In other words, they are used to obstruct the sun from shining on a particular area. They dim or darken areas that otherwise would be illuminated by the sun. Joshua told the people before you can live in this region you must eliminate all the things that are preventing you from clearly seeing this new land.

God has some new aspirations, new activities, new positions, and new desires he wants you to grasp, but before you can get them you must cut down the trees of doubt and fear that are blocking you from fully seeing the expanded blessings of God. God is trying to illuminate your future and give you a clear view of what he has for you, but some of you walk among the trees of doubt and fear and God's new blessings are being placed in shadows. Cut down the trees so that the sun may shine on the land.

The Manassites were not simply commanded to cut down the trees but also to make the land clear. Even if you cut down a tree, a stump still remains. As long as the stump is in the ground one will not be able to build on the land. Jeremiah 1:10 says, "See, today I appoint you over the nations and kingdoms to uproot and tear down...." Luke 17:6 proclaims, "If you have faith as small as a mustard seed, you can say to this mulberry tree, 'Be uprooted and planted in the sea and it will obey you.' "

Even a stump of doubt and fear can prevent you from possessing the expanded blessings that God has for you. Your doubt and fear must be uprooted if you want to live on the new blessings of God.

One Tree Missing

The Manassites went into the forest and saw a gargantuan hole in the ground that extended the width of the entire forest. After examining the hole for a while they realized that a tree once occupied the hole, but someone had cut it down and uprooted it. When they saw that someone was able to cut down and remove a tree that big, they realized the rest of the trees in the forest would not be as difficult to uproot. They received hope that they could clear the forest with this head start.

One colossal tree has been cut down for you and me. On this tree, Jesus cleared away all our sins. As you prepare to live in the new territory that God has created for you, acknowledge and embrace the one who removed the most important tree of all — the tree of sin. Then clear out the land and its farthest limits will be yours.

Prayer

Everlasting provider, you promised to care for all our needs. When our world shifts, the demands in our lives increase and resources become depleted, you are able to expand our territory. Let us stand boldly upon the new blessings that you have given us, even before others acknowledge our divine ownership. Amen.

Relevant Questions And Sermon Points

How Do We Outgrow Our Blessings?
1. Claim what God has already given you.
2. Recognize when your context is no longer adequate for you based on God's plan.
3. Cut down and uproot doubts and fears that prevent you from seeing new blessings.

Questions For Individual Reflection Or Group Discussion

1. List four people, both past and present, who are responsible for something you possess effortlessly now. How often do you honor or thank these people?

2. What are some things that you believe God wants you to do, but you have yet to do them? What is preventing you from doing them?

3. What are some steps that you need to take to move into the "land" that God has for you?

4. How do you determine when a relationship, place, or environment becomes "too small" for you?

5. What are some fears and doubts you have about trying something new based on God's prompting? How can these fears and doubts be cut down and uprooted?

Renew Faith

So Elijah said, "Go and tell Ahab, 'Hitch up your chariot and go down before the rain stops you.' "
— 1 Kings 18:44

How did we get here? This is one of the most perplexing questions that each of us will have to face again and again throughout our lives.

- "We used to love each other and want to spend every waking moment together. But now all we do is argue and we can't stand to be around each other. How did we get here?"
- "She was so precious as a baby. She never gave us any trouble. But now she contests everything we say. She doesn't listen or respect us. Our child is no longer pleasant to be around. How did we get here?"
- "I was so excited about starting this job. It was a great opportunity for me. But now I dread going into work. My supervisor doesn't care for me. My work is monotonous. How did I get here?"
- "I was thrilled about starting my first day of school. I couldn't wait to see what this new environment would be like. But now I don't even want to go to class. All the assignments I receive are a burden. How did I get here?"
- "We couldn't wait to move into our new home. The neighborhood was perfect. The layout of the house was great. But now the house seems too small. The neighbors don't seem so considerate. How did we get here?"
- "I was looking forward to retirement and all that I could do. I eagerly expected the time off and freedom I would enjoy.

But now I am contemplating going back to work. My weekends are not as enjoyable as they used to be. How did I get here?"

We often ask ourselves, "How can something that started out so good, fresh, and promising end up so miserable, painful, and sad? What happened between then and now to cause me to get here? How did I get here?"

Elijah posed the same question to the nation of Israel. He said, "At one time you put your complete faith in Yahweh. You gladly sacrificed to the Lord and brought your offerings to the temple with joy. You prayed every day and read God's law. But now you have wandered off and accepted other gods. You don't sacrifice like you did. Now you grudgingly bring your tithes and offerings to the temple. You don't have time to read God's word and pray. How did we get to a place of apathy and disbelief? How did we get here?"

More Than One God Now

Our passage gives us some indication about how the Israelites fall into their present spiritual condition. Baal and Asherah were companion deities. Baal was the god of the storm and Asherah was the goddess of the sea. Jezebel was a foreigner who married the Israelite King Ahab. Once she became queen, she began to give her gods a prominent place in Israelite society. Yahweh was no longer the only viable option to serve.

We have come to a place in society where a Christian way of life is no longer the only option. There was a time when even if a person did not accept the Christian lifestyle, you were at least a marginal Christian. He or she would fake it and do the bare minimum. In today's world, people do not even lie anymore. They will tell you to your face, "I think church is useless. I don't believe in Jesus' divinity. I don't practice formal religion, it is too restrictive." There are other belief systems, philosophies, and lifestyles that have been validated by our culture as acceptable and legitimate.

Elijah said, "Now that you have all these other viable options, pick one. Don't keep on vacillating among all of them." Sometimes the Israelites called out Yahweh's name and sometimes that of Baal. Sometimes they acted like a believer and other times they acted like skeptics. Sometimes they brought their tithes and offerings to the temple and other times kept them for themselves. Sometimes they had time to make sacrifices for God but other times they were too busy. Sometimes they wanted to be holy and devout and other times they wanted to boldly sin. Sometimes they wanted to be loving and kind but other times they wanted to be mean and spiteful.

Sometimes we want to be Christians, but other times we want to forget our Christian lifestyles. Similar to the Israelites, we cannot be a people of faith simply when it is convenient for us, and then when something else is more convenient, easier, or appealing we immediately go there. God calls us to remain consistent in our faith.

Missing Element — Fire

Elijah said to the other prophets, "Let's prepare a sacrifice. I will prepare one to Yahweh and you will prepare one to your gods. Get the bull, the wood, and place everything on your altar, but do not start a fire under it. I will do the same for my sacrifice." Elijah wanted the prophets to prepare a sacrifice, but leave the most crucial element of the sacrifice — the fire — missing. Then Elijah said, "After we have prepared our sacrifices without the fire, we will see whose god can provide the missing element to the sacrifice."

The prophets of Baal prepared their sacrifice and petitioned their god to provide the fire. After they danced around the altar, shouted at the top of their voices, and cut themselves, what they needed was still missing.

Some of us called out to the god of wealth. We tried to obtain as many material possessions as possible. We received the big house, the new car, the promotion, the large savings account, and the pension plan, but there was still something missing. Some of us called out to the god of love. We received our mate. We received our family and kids, but there was still something missing. Some of us went out and called out to the god of intellect. We received our degrees. We received our titles. We received new knowledge and understanding, but there was still something missing. Some of us called out to the god of good deeds. We helped people. We donated money. We took time out of our schedules to make other people's lives better, but there was still something missing. We still lacked the fire.

After the prophets attempted to have Baal provide the missing piece, Elijah received his turn. In Elijah's attempt to petition Yahweh, we get some indication as to how to renew our faith.

Rebuilt Altar

Elijah took twelve stones that represented the twelve founding tribes of Israel to build his altar. He thought of the memories and feelings when Israel received its identity as a people of faith.

There was a teenage girl who went to visit her grandmother for a week. The first night at her grandmother's house she slept soundly and awoke early in the morning. Not accustomed to being awake so early, the girl decided to make a cup of tea and read the newspaper until her grandmother arose. The girl went to the kitchen, found a kettle, poured some water in it, placed it on the stove, turned on the stove, and went into the living room to read her paper. Three minutes passed and the aroma of bacon and cinnamon reached the girl's nose. Startled, she went into the kitchen and looked on the stove. Present on the stove was the kettle she left there. The girl opened the oven to see if anything was in there, but found nothing. She looked on every counter top and section of the kitchen, but could not identify from where this aroma of bacon and cinnamon was coming.

An hour later, the grandmother came down to the kitchen. The girl gave her grandmother her standard morning kiss and hug. As the grandmother began to pour water in the kettle to make a cup of tea, the granddaughter said, "Grandma, when I was boiling some water in the kettle, I smelled this aroma of bacon and cinnamon, but I could not find from where it was coming." The grandmother responded, "Which burner did you use, baby?" "This one here on the right," she said. The grandmother slowly nodded her head and said, "Two days before you came here I cooked some bacon and

French toast on that burner. The aroma that you smell is from the remnants of that meal."

Even if we lack faith, we can still smell the aroma of those who had a faith stronger than ours. If we really want to renew our faith, we must revisit those places, experiences, and people. We must go back to where the faith began. We must go back to a man named Jesus, who lived a perfect and righteous life and was crucified. We must go back to a woman named Mary, who sat beside the resurrected Christ and said, "Teacher, is that you?" We must go back to the disciples who were locked in a room and excited because they just saw their risen master. We must go back to the road of Damascus, where a person named Saul, who hated all Christians, saw Jesus and was never the same. We must go back to that grandmother or grandfather who had faith in Christ that carried them through thick and thin. We have to go back to those places, people, and experiences that force us to say, "There has to be something to this Jesus Christ character. I don't know exactly what, but there is no way this many people could have made this many sacrifices if there wasn't."

Pours Water On Sacrifice

Elijah prepared his altar, but when he prepared it he poured water over the altar, the wood, and the sacrifice. He placed something in the equation that made the sacrifice less likely to catch on fire. He put something on his sacrifice that would have made everyone watching doubt that the sacrifice could catch on fire.

If we want to renew our faith in Christ, we must bring all our doubts to the table. Doubt is essential for belief. Without the existence of some doubt there can be no belief. What makes belief so powerful is the fact that some people doubt it.

Prayed And Believed

Elijah had four large jars filled with reasons to doubt that the sacrifice would catch on fire. He had a trench filled with reasons why the sacrifice would not catch on fire. In the midst of his doubt, and in the midst of all the reasons why the sacrifice would not catch on fire, Elijah prayed to God and believed that the missing piece would be provided. Elijah prayed and believed when he was surrounded by doubt.

In order for Christ to fulfill this missing piece, you must believe even when you do not see any reason why you should. This is the only way that you will receive the fire.

Moses was convinced that God had called him to lead the Israelites once he saw a bush that was on fire but was not being consumed. The Israelites knew that God was with them and would protect them in the wilderness because they had a pillar of fire that led them throughout the night. The early Christian community was affirmed of Jesus' divinity and Messianic place when the Holy Spirit descended upon them at Pentecost like tongues of fire. An encounter with fire is the confirmation that someone receives when they are in the right place and are within the presence of God. In order to receive the fire, the absolute conviction in Jesus, you must believe in the midst of doubt. Romans 10:11 states, "Anyone who trusts in him will never be put to shame."

Rain Comes

Once the people received the fire, the drought came to an end. The rain that was to come was going to be so strong that Elijah sent word to Ahab to go into his palace before the rain stops him. Once we have the conviction of Christ within us and give our hearts to Christ the world that seemed so barren, meaningless, and lackluster becomes full of possibility and hope. Malachi 3:10 states, " 'Test me in this,' says the Lord almighty, 'and see if I will not throw open the floodgates of heaven and pour out so much blessings that you will not have room enough for it.' " Turn back your hearts to Christ on this day and observe how your life will change.

Prayer

Everlasting redeemer, you are faithful even when our faith falters. Your loving presence is extended to us even when fears prevent us from walking closer to you. Surround us with your steadfast servants so that we may always be reminded of the tremendous security and peace found in you. May our doubts become springboards for renewed faith in your promises. Amen.

Relevant Questions And Sermon Points

How Can We Renew Our Faith?
1. Revisit those people who lived faithful lives.
2. Bring all your doubts into the open.
3. Believe in the midst of those doubts.

Questions For Individual Reflection Or Group Discussion

1. What are some missing elements in your spiritual life?

2. Who are some people that you believe best exemplify a life of faith? What can you take to feel closer to them?

3. List your greatest doubts regarding your faith, either present or past.

4. Can you remember a time when you believed something contrary to all the evidence available? How did you feel? Why did you choose to have faith?

Open Eyes Of Faith

When the servant of the man of God got up and went out early the next morning, an army with horses and chariots had surrounded the city.   — 2 Kings 6:15

By this particular point in the book of Kings, Elisha had become the most influential prophet in the land. He was no longer that little boy who followed his master, Elijah, from place to place. He was now the one who made the pronouncements, prophecies, and judgments to the rulers. He was the one who the people of Israel sought after to heal their water. He was the one who allowed the widow's oil to expand and brought back to life the wealthy woman's son. He was the one who cured the pot of food that was not edible and miraculously fed those without enough food. He was the one who cured Naaman of his leprosy. He was now the head prophet in charge, the undisputed spiritual leader of Israel. From this position of authority, Elisha told three parties, "Open your eyes of faith."

Israel Is Under Attack

The king of Aram, for no apparent reason, declared war on Israel, the people of God, and began to develop battle strategies to defeat them. As Christians, we must become astute enough to know when we are under spiritual attack. "Be self-controlled and alert. Your enemy the devil prowls around like a roaring lion looking for someone to devour" (1 Peter 5:8). "For our struggle is not against flesh and blood, but against the rulers, against the authorities, against the powers of this dark world and against spiritual forces of evil in the heavenly realms" (Ephesians 6:12).

More than a third of Jesus' healings dealt with direct confrontation of demonic forces. The very first question that *The United*

Methodist Hymnal asks parents who bring their child to be baptized is "Do you renounce the spiritual forces of wickedness?" Some of you may be thinking, "I don't believe in demonic forces. I have never seen any evidence of them." If you are in this category either one of two situations have occurred. One, you have misinterpreted the factors at play in your life. You had days, months, or years in which you thought you were just having a difficult time. You thought that you had just encountered some cold, rude people and had been in some unfriendly environments. Actually you were in the midst of spiritual warfare and did not even know it. The other people, environments, as well as you and your household were under spiritual attack during those times in your life.

The second reason why some might be in that category is because they have become so self-absorbed and consumed with the things of this world that they are not even worthy of the devil's attention. If you want to be convinced of spiritual warfare, then leave your door and start telling someone about Jesus Christ — I dare you.

As Christians we must recognize that the dilemmas in our society are not simply a matter of greed, violence, corruption, or prejudice, but are spiritual in their every essence. We will never be able to completely eradicate many of the dilemmas in our society until we address the spiritual components of them.

Elisha Addresses His Servant

The first party that Elisha addressed was his servant. Each time the king of Aram wanted to attack and destroy Israel, Elisha warned and prepared Israel for the attack and frustrated the king's plans. After a number of unsuccessful attempts, the king discovered the cause of his failure and sent men to capture Elisha.

One morning Elisha's servant arose, washed his face, and began his daily routine. He expected the day to be a normal one. As the servant gingerly walked past the city gate he noticed that the city was surrounded by men positioned to do his master and him harm. The servant ran to Elisha and told him what was occurring and Elisha responded, "Open your eyes of faith."

This servant was most likely an apprentice under Elisha. He was a prophet in training. Elisha told this servant, "If you ever want to become a prophet like me you must begin to see what cannot be seen."

There are two types of faith that we must highlight. The first type of faith is the general faith that all Christians possess in varying degrees. This type of faith allows you to have confidence and know that there are unseen and undetected factors present that will assist you and others. This is the type of faith that the servant had. He believed in God's power. He knew God would make a way. He just didn't see how it would be made possible.

However, there is a second type of faith where not only do you know that there are unseen factors involved, but you can see some of these factors, which no one else can see. Elisha told his servant "If you ever want to become a leader you must cultivate a spiritual maturity and intimacy with God that allows you to see the unseen."

In order for us to build the kingdom of God on earth, we must be able to see what is not visible. We must have a vision that is greater and broader than the people who do not know Christ. One of the reasons why our mainline Protestant denominations are in drastic decline is because we have lost our insight into the spiritual nature of this world. Far too often there is no difference between what we see and what a non-believer sees. Can you imagine what type of leader and witness Elisha would have been had he not seen anything different? Do you think anyone would have ever been convicted to follow the Lord if Elisha simply saw the world the way everyone else did?

Elisha Addresses The Army

The second party that Elisha addressed was the men sent by the king to capture him. Once Elisha saw these men approaching, he prayed to the Lord for them to be blinded. These men were already blind because they could not see the chariots and horses of the Lord that were waiting to defend Elisha. But Elisha prayed that these men would become blind to even what they could see because this was only way they would heed his commands.

The Lord made Saul blind in order for Saul to listen to the Lord's voice. Samson became weak and blind before he realized that his power came from the Lord. Our Christian growth starts from an acknowledgment that we do not know all the answers. We do not understand everything. We don't know the right way. We don't know the proper destination. Our Christian growth can only start from an acknowledgment that we are blind, and we must follow the voice of God to find our way.

There was a husband and wife who decided to travel to the beach for a weekend. They talked with some of their friends about how to get to this one particular beach. Once the weekend arrived, they had a general idea of how to get there and off they went. After traveling on a major highway for almost an hour, they came to an exit they believed they were supposed to take but were not sure. They discussed it for a moment, but the decision had to be made quickly. The husband finally took the exit and said, "I think this is the right one."

The highway placed the couple onto a smaller road. As soon as they were deposited on this smaller road, the wife said, "Maybe we should stop here and ask for directions." The husband responded, "No, I think that was the right exit. We will be fine." The couple drove a little further and the small road on which they traveled became a dirt road. Once the wife noticed the change in pavement, she said, "I think we should stop here and ask for directions." The husband responded, "We are fine. That tree and bird right there look familiar. We're okay." They continued on the dirt road and a storm emerged. The rain began to pound on the windshield and the wife became even more worried. "I think we should stop right here and ask for directions," the wife said. The husband shook his head, "That is why we have windshield wipers — for rain and storms like this one."

They journeyed through the storm, but the rain caused the road to become muddy and mud smeared onto the windshield, which made the windshield even less transparent. "I think we should stop here and ask for directions," the wife repeated in a tone of frustration. The husband chose not to respond this time. With the hindered vision and rough road, the husband ran over a small ditch that punctured the front tire. Their car eventually rolled to a stop. With mud covering the windshield, rain pouring down, and a flat tire, the husband turned to the wife and said, "I think I am going to stop here and ask for directions." Sometimes we must be placed in total darkness before we can acknowledge that we need assistance.

Elisha led the men to Samaria and said to them, "Open your eyes of faith," and the men saw that they were surrounded by the people of God. Once you acknowledge that you are blind and listen for God's voice to find your way, you will be able to see how God's grace is (and was) with you throughout your journey. You must become blind in order to see and grow in Christ. Once you acknowledge that you cannot see and then follow God, your vision becomes better than before.

Elisha Addresses The King Of Israel

The last party that Elisha addressed was the king of Israel. Once the king of Israel saw the men sent by the king of Aram, he asked Elisha if the Israelites should eliminate them. Elisha's response was, "Open your eyes of faith and see that these men are hungry."

As Christian disciples we must stop seeing non-believers and people of no faith as different and opposed to us. We must open our eyes of faith and see them as in need of a type of nourishment that only Christ can provide. We must offer non-believers at least three types of food. One, we must offer them an invitation to become changed by Jesus Christ. John 6:35 says, "Jesus declared, 'I am the bread of life. He who comes to me will never go hungry and he who believes in me will never be thirsty.' " Two, we must offer them an invitation to know God's word. Matthew 4:4 states, "It is written: 'Man does not live on bread alone, but on every word that comes from the mouth of God.' " Three, we must offer them an invitation to serve God. Jesus proclaims, "My food is to do the will of him who sent me and to finish his work" (John 4:34).

Men Of Aram Are Fed And Released

After they were fed, some of the men did not leave. They probably said to one another, "If this is how Israel treats their enemies,

I want to be a part of this nation. They have fed us when we were in need and vulnerable." Some left and returned. They noticed the meaning and intentionality in which the people of God lived their lives, and they yearned for another meal from these people and their God. The majority of the men went back to Aram and told their country members how the people of God fed them. Their encounter with Israel was transformed into a living testimony in a foreign land.

We must open our eyes of faith to see that God desires us to see the unseen; God's grace surrounds us, and all who do not know Christ are in need of a type of spiritual nourishment that only the church and Christian believers can provide.

Prayer

Merciful Savior, close our eyes so that we may see. Shut our mouths so that you may speak. Open our hearts so that we may listen. Amen.

Relevant Questions And Sermon Points

What Will The Eyes Of Faith Show Us?
1. The eyes of faith will show you what is not visible.
2. They will show you darkness.
3. They will show that people are in need of God.

Questions For Individual Reflection Or Group Discussion

1. Identify a period in your life or a particular encounter when you may have been under spiritual attack. What made this experience unique?

2. Can your faith journey be summarized as being able to see the unseen, seeing darkness, or seeing the need of God in others? Why?

3. Which is the most difficult for you to experience: seeing the unseen, seeing darkness, or seeing others' need for God? Why?

4. What insight has God revealed to you through this scripture?

Mature In Christ

The Spirit told Philip, "Go to that chariot and stay near it." Then Philip ran up to the chariot and heard the man reading Isaiah the prophet.   — Acts 8:29-30

The disciples walked the earth with Christ for about three years. During that time they accumulated a lot of insightful parables. They saw a lot of miraculous events. They learned a lot about the scriptures. They gained the ability to heal the sick. By the time their three years had passed, they were more spiritually mature than they had ever been. Jesus looked at his disciples before he departed and said, "Now that you have all this insight, now that you have seen God's intervention time and time again, now that you know the scriptures a little better, now that you have gained the ability to heal the sick, now that you are more spiritually mature than you have ever been, 'Go into all the world and preach the good news to all creation' " (Mark 16:15). Jesus told his disciples that the reason why they had become spiritually mature was so they could go out and tell others about the gospel.

Similar to the other disciples, Philip had undergone some significant spiritual growth. In Acts 6, Philip was distributing food to the Jewish and Hebraic widows. By Acts 8 we learn that Philip was not only distributing food, but also began to tell others in Samaria about Christ. Between chapter 6 and chapter 8, enough spiritual growth had occurred in Philip to move him from a believer who was quiet and reserved to a believer who told everyone he encountered about Jesus. In Philip's encounter with the Ethiopian eunuch we see some signs of spiritual maturity displayed.

Philip Goes South

An angel came to Philip and said, "Philip, get on that desert road and go south." The angel did not give Philip an address to go to. He did not print out any directions from Mapquest. He did not give Philip a particular place in the road to stop. He did not tell Philip to look for any particular person on the road. He said, "Philip, go south." With all that uncertainty and ambiguity looming, Philip went south.

A sign of spiritual maturity in Christ is when you do not need all the details to follow God's plan. God has some destinations for you, but God also has some journeys for you. When God sends you on a journey, you do not need to know the destination because the destination involves having the faith to go on the journey.

While Philip traveled south, he saw an Ethiopian eunuch who was a high official for the queen of Ethiopia. This eunuch was coming back from worship in Jerusalem and was reading the book of Isaiah.

Whenever you see Ethiopia in the Bible it usually refers to the region of Cush or the upper Nile region. This area is most aligned with modern-day Sudan. A eunuch was a male who could not pro-create; therefore, eunuchs were usually obtained to work with the women in royal courts. This particular eunuch was a treasurer in the royal palace of the Cush kingdom. The Spirit of God prompts Philip to stand beside this eunuch's chariot. Notice again that Philip was not given any particular details of what to do once he arrived at the chariot.

Philip Listens

Philip went to the chariot of the eunuch and did not begin to preach or teach, but instead he listened to the voice reading the book of Isaiah in the chariot. James 1:19 tells us, "Everyone should be quick to listen, slow to speak." A spiritually mature person in Christ first listens for opportunities to tell others about Christ before speaking. You must understand or have an idea of where a person is before you can proclaim Christ to them.

This eunuch was reading the book of Isaiah. The eunuch was at a place in his life where he was trying to discover God's salvation through the book of Isaiah. Once we listen and observe people's emotional states, physical states, relationships, goals, and aspirations we will find in all of them some type of attempt to get to a better place. We will find some type of attempt to rescue themselves from where they are and get closer to God (whether they realize it or not). This eunuch was in the book of Isaiah and from there he tried to get to a better place; he tried to get closer to God, but he did not know how. Our passage then informs us, "Then Philip began with that very passage of scripture and told him the good news about Jesus" (Acts 8:35). Philip started with the book of Isaiah and then showed the eunuch how it connected to Christ. By bringing the eunuch to Christ, he was able to bring the eunuch to this desired place — closer to God.

Spiritual maturity in Christ occurs when you understand that bringing people closer to God means introducing them to Christ.

There was a homeless man who developed a routine for survival in his city. He would frequent three places within the same block to sustain himself on the streets. First, he would go to a restaurant to beg for leftovers. Then, the homeless man went to a high-end clothing store and asked customers for spare change in front of the store. Last, the man would position himself near a vent beside a hotel to keep warm at night.

One day while the homeless man stood begging for leftovers in front of the restaurant, a wealthy man saw him and asked if he would like to eat with him inside the restaurant. The homeless man responded, "They will never let me in there. Look at me." The wealthy man said, "Don't worry, just follow directly behind me." The wealthy man went into the restaurant and the homeless man followed directly behind him. As soon as the homeless man entered, the hostess ran over to him and said, "Excuse me, but you cannot come in here." The wealthy man pulled the hostess aside and whispered something in her ear and then the hostess waved the homeless man to come into the restaurant.

The wealthy man and homeless man left the restaurant and the wealthy man said, "I had planned on buying a new coat from that store on the corner. Would you like to come with me and I could buy you a few items of clothing that you may need?" The homeless man laughed, "They will never allow me in that store. The security guards don't even allow me to stand in front of the store and panhandle on most days." The wealthy man said, "Don't worry about it. Just follow directly behind me." The wealthy man entered the store and the homeless man followed directly behind him. As soon as the homeless man entered the store, the security guard grabbed him and said, "Excuse me, but you cannot be in here." The wealthy man pulled the security guard to the side, whispered something in his ear, and the security guard nodded his head and allowed the homeless man to enter the store.

After they left the store, the wealthy man said, "I am staying at a hotel on this same block, would you like to take a shower there?" "I know exactly the hotel you are referring to. They will never let me in there," said the homeless man. "Don't worry about it. Just followed directly behind me," the wealthy man replied. The wealthy man entered the hotel and the homeless man followed directly behind him. As soon as the homeless man walked into the lobby, the attendant came to him and said, "Excuse me sir, you cannot be here." The wealthy man pulled the attendant aside, whispered something in his ear, and the attendant nodded his head and allowed the homeless man to proceed.

Once the homeless man had taken his shower and put on his new clothes he felt like a new man. As the homeless man left the hotel he shook the wealthy man's hand and said, "Thank you so much for feeding me, clothing me, and allowing me to clean up. You will never know how much I appreciate it. But I have one question for you." "Sure, what is it?" the wealthy man replied. "Each time we entered a place together and someone stopped me, you would go over to that person and whisper something in their ear. What did you say to them?" the homeless man said curiously. "I simply told them that you were with me," the wealthy man replied.

There were some places that we never had access to. There were some relationships, degrees of authenticity, levels of consciousness and compassion, forms of discernment, and states of peace that we were never able to access. Jesus came along and said, "I can take you to those places, just follow directly behind me," and some of us followed. When we began to enter these places God looked at us and said, "They are not loving enough, they are not smart enough, they are not conscious enough, they are not compassionate enough, they are not peaceful enough, they don't deserve to be here." But Jesus pulled God aside and said, "They are with me."

As Christians we believe that the way we become closer to God is through Christ. This is why we end all prayers in Christ's name. We come closer to God in a natural sense because we now have a model to follow to do God's will. But we also come closer to God in a spiritual sense because once we accept Christ as the way, God no longer sees our inadequacies. Our shortcomings are covered by Christ's sacrifice for us. Christ is the bridge between humanity and divinity. Christ actualizes God to humanity.

Philip Baptizes The Eunuch

Philip baptized the eunuch. Baptism signifies the formal entrance into the Christian community. A sign of Christian maturity is when you begin to incorporate others into the Christian community. One will never be able to understand and know Christ intimately if he or she is separated from the Christian community because the Christian community is the body of Christ.

Our spiritual maturity in Christ leads us to one place — sharing and spreading the good news about Jesus Christ. As we mature in Christ, we should become more comfortable, more inspired, and more creative in sharing the gospel with others.

Prayer

All-knowing God, you are the creator of the master blueprint for our lives. Even though we do not fully know your plans, we trust in your ability. Despite our inability to see outcomes, we have faith in your vision. Through a discerning spirit, may we become one with your will. Amen.

Relevant Questions And Sermon Points

How Can We Become Mature In Christ?
1. Follow God even when you do not know the details.
2. Listen first for opportunities to tell others about Christ.
3. Share the good news of Jesus Christ with others.

Questions For Individual Reflection Or Group Discussion

1. Think of one recent instance that represents your growth in Christ? Share with the group.

2. Have you ever acted based on the prompting of the Holy Spirit without knowing the details about where you were going? What occurred? How did you feel?

3. Do you find great difficulty in waiting for opportunities to speak about Christ or greater difficulty to tell others about Christ? Why?

4. Can you remember a moment when you told someone else about Christ? How did you feel? What occurred?

Shout The News

When they reached the edge of the camp, not a man was there, for the Lord had caused the Arameans to hear the sound of chariots and horses and a great army.
— 2 Kings 7:5-6

As we grow older, we are more predisposed to possess suspicion and even skepticism of any claims that seem remarkable. The longer we travel on this journey called life, the more probable we are to think and verbalize the statement, "That is too good to be true." When a woman walks down the grocery store aisle and sees all these age-defying products that guarantee she will look twenty years younger, she will say, "That is too good to be true." When a man is sitting in front of the television late at night and an infomercial appears promoting new exercise equipment, which claims he will look like the body builder who is using it, he will say, "That is too good to be true." When we see political candidates that declare they will cut taxes and also increase spending on the vital needs of society, we say, "That is too good to be true." When we hear about the latest diet, which proposes that all we need is to do one simple thing and we can lose as much weight as we want, we will say, "That is too good to be true."

Even though our suspicion and skepticism have equipped us with the ability to identify all these claims that cannot be true, there is still something deep inside of us that wants to believe them. No matter how many beauty products we have seen produce nominal or no results, we still want to believe that the next one will work. No matter how many exercise products we have tried and have failed at making exercise easy, we still want to believe one can do the work for us. No matter how many political candidates have disappointed us, we still want to believe that one can do all that they say they can do. No matter how many diet fads come and go, we still want to be believe that one diet will allow us to eat what we want and lose weight at the same time. No matter how much we claim that some things are too good to be true, there is a part of us that wants to believe that something is good and true.

The reason why you cannot let go of this lingering notion within you is because your spirit knows that there is something similar out there. Your spirit has been telling you all your life that there is something out there that is spectacular, remarkable, good, and true. So you went searching for it in your body image, conception of beauty, and in the political and financial realms. You went searching for something that you knew was out there, but you could not find it in those places.

The moment you enter into a personal relationship with Jesus Christ your life will be transformed. I know it sounds remarkable. I know it sounds spectacular. I know it sounds unbelievable. I know it sounds too good to be true, but it is good and true.

The issue that we will examine is not the claim that Jesus Christ will transform your life, but the various positions that we can take to this claim. In this passage of 2 Kings we see three positions that one can take in reference to something that is good and true.

Donkey Heads And Seedpods Increase In Value
Samaria, the capital of northern Israel, had been attacked. During the attack, the people were prevented from leaving their city and replenishing their food supply. In this context where food was lacking, a donkey head and a cab of seedpods or dove dung became valuable. In the normal state of affairs, donkey heads were not eaten. When a donkey died it was disposed of. Seedpods or dove dung contained little nutritional value. What was normally discarded and of low nutritional worth had now become valuable in the context of a famine.

We have arrived at a point in our society where the opinions and thoughts of talk show hosts, singers, actors, actresses, and politicians have become overvalued and inflated in worth because the word of God is no longer prevalent. "The days are coming," declares the sovereign Lord, "when I will send a famine through the land — not a famine of food or a thirst for water, but a famine of hearing the words of the Lord" (Amos 8:11). When the unadulterated word of God stops being taught and preached in our schools, homes, society, and even in our churches, people start to look for spiritual nourishment in popular culture. Even though the book written by that model, actor, singer, or celebrity might only have a morsel of insight, it rises in value when the word of God is absent.

Staple Food Will Be Available

Bread was a staple food in ancient Israel. It was one of the most basic elements of the meal. Bread was usually made from barley or wheat. Bread made from wheat was more expensive; therefore, not everyone could obtain it, but bread made from barley could be purchased by the very poorest of society. Elisha said that in a very short period of time sustainable food would be available that everyone can obtain.

First Position
Officer Doubts Elisha's Claim

The assistant to the king heard this claim that Israel would go from scraps to substantial food overnight and said, "That is too good to be true." He could not figure out how this could occur; therefore, he did not accept the claim. The assistant said, "Based on the time it takes to pick barley grain, separate the chaff, grind it in the mills to produce flour, and distribute it to the people, how could this occur? Even if grain and flour were imported from another place, I don't see how they will be able to get through the Aramean army. I'm sorry Elisha, but I just can't figure out how that claim could be true."

The first position that we can take to the claim that Christ transforms lives is a theoretical one. We could say, "Based on the different psychological and sociological factors preventing a person from being transformed, I can't figure out how Christ could do it. Based on all the different belief systems and ways of living, I can't see how Christ can make that much of a difference."

The funny thing about God is that God has a tendency to accomplish something in a way that we would have never considered. God told the Israelites, "You are going to conquer the city of Jericho." The Israelites responded, "There is no way we can conquer that city because the people are so strong and skilled at fighting." God responded, "Who said anything about fighting? I want you to walk around the walls seven times and blow your trumpets." God told Moses, "I am going to provide the people with some water." Moses said, "We are in the desert and would have to travel for miles before we could get any water." God said, "Who said anything about traveling? Hit the rock with your staff and water will come forth." Jesus determined that he was going to get more wine for the banquet. The servants said, "All the stores are closed." Jesus said, "Who said anything about going to the store? I will change that water into wine." God does not need you to understand how the claim will be manifested — he just needs you to believe it.

This assistant missed out on something that was too good and true because he wanted to approach the claim from a theoretical position. Notice something very briefly. This assistant was in a place of privilege. He was the king's assistant. Although there was not much food left, he would always have what was available because he was in the palace. Some doubt and speculation is a luxury that only the privileged of society can afford to possess. When you think you will have a meal, shelter, and safety, it is much easier to speculate and question God's goodness.

Second Position
King Doubts The Claim
The king heard the news that substantial food was both available and abundant, and then stated, "That is too good to be true — it must be a trap." The king said, "In all my years on the throne I have never encountered anything like this. I have never experienced any enemy just up and leave when they were on the verge of a victory. This just doesn't happen." The king's prior experience would not let him accept the claim.

The second position that we can take to the claim that Jesus transforms lives is an experiential one. The transformation that occurs when you enter into a personal relationship with Christ is like no other experience that you have ever had. If you are comparing your prior experience to the claim that Jesus transforms lives you will never be able to accept it.

Third Position
Lepers Surrender
Four men, who possessed leprosy, stood at the city gate contemplating what they should do in the context of this famine. They said, "If we stay where we are we are going to die; if we go back to where we came from we are going to die; let's try something that we have never done before and surrender to the Arameans. Maybe they will spare us and feed us. Maybe we will encounter something too good and true."

The third position that you can take in reference to the claim that Jesus transforms lives is one of surrender. Some of us are in a crossroads in our life. We can keep on doing what we are doing, which is not working. We can go back to doing what we have done, which was not working. Or we can try something that we have never done before — surrender to the possibility that entering into a relationship with Christ will change our lives.

Signs Of Someone Who Has Surrendered
The lepers revealed three signs of someone who had surrendered. First, the lepers had their needs met as soon as they walked onto the Arameans' camp. Even though they had only reached the edge or the outer limit of the camp, they received food, clothing, and treasures. When you surrender to Christ, you will discover some immediate satisfaction and fulfillment that you were not aware of. You will still have struggles and difficult periods, but a fundamental change emerges once you make that decision.

Once the lepers reached the camp of the Arameans, they found it was abandoned. The lepers had no idea how this Aramean camp became deserted and *they did not care* how it became deserted. When you surrender to Christ you will become more comfortable

81

with the mystery of God. There will be many times in your life when you cannot understand how something happened or why something did or did not happen. Once you surrender to Christ, you find comfort in the fact that God is God, whether you understand the situation or not.

Lastly, the lepers could not fully enjoy the plunder of the Aramean camp until they told the rest of Samaria. They were determined to share the good news about what they had found. When one truly surrenders to Christ, that transformation is so profound that he or she wants everyone else to also experience it. We must tell others about the good news of Jesus Christ. It makes our salvation even more enjoyable.

Conclusion

What Jesus Christ can do for you is spectacular and remarkable. It is the one thing that you have been searching for your entire life that is too good and true.

Prayer

Heavenly Father, we draw ourselves closer to thee. To be known by you is better than possessing the mysteries of the universe. Each step we take toward you exposes us to a new sense of peace. As we grow in you, may your Spirit grow out of us to reach the world. Amen.

Relevant Questions And Sermon Points

What Are The Signs We Have Surrendered To Christ?
1. Immediate sense of peace.
2. More comfort with the mystery of God.
3. Determined to share Christ with others.

Questions For Individual Reflection Or Group Discussion

1. What are some things that you think are overvalued and undervalued in our society? Why do you think this is the case?

2. Do you think the word of God could be made more prevalent in our society? How?

3. Do you respond to the promises of God like the king's assistant, the king, or the lepers? Identify one particular instance that is most indicative of your responses. What are the main factors that trigger this type of response?

4. Identify one aspect of your life that requires surrendering. What makes surrendering so difficult or easy in this aspect?

5. What insight has God revealed to you through this scripture?

Conclusion

Sometimes we are full-time chariot chasers. We are similar to Elijah's servants as we chase a chariot that we think possesses the "good old days." A fear of change causes us to pursue the things of the past at any cost. Sometimes we are like Gehazi, chasing a chariot out of greed and self-righteousness. What we believe people deserve pushes us to seek revenge and rectify all that is out of order. Sometimes we are like Barak, who chased a chariot that he falsely assumed was essential to his success. Many of us have acquired positions or resources that we think will satisfy us, but we still feel empty. Sometimes we are like Israel who requested a king riding in a chariot so she could be like the other nations. What others have and do appears so appealing until we finally possess and are doing those same things. Chasing after chariots can consume many of us. In different moments we can identify with Naaman, who almost allowed his elevated, comfortable position in a chariot to prevent him from being healed. Too easily we can become grounded in the security and luxury that this world provides.

Other times the chariots are chasing us. Similar to the Israelites, who were terrorized by the Egyptian and Canaanite chariots, we fear advancing forward because of those things that seek to destroy us. When we are opposed by overwhelming forces, we believe our only option is to run for our lives.

Chariots can also be instruments of the divine. As a result of Philip chasing a chariot, an Ethiopian eunuch came to know Christ.

The heavenly chariots that surrounded Elijah and his servant was confirmation to the people of God that "Those who are with us are more than those who are [against us]." Sometimes chariots have no other purpose than to be vehicles to tell the good news of God's deliverance.

Will the chariots in your life strengthen or hinder your relationship with God? I pray that you will chase chariots when the gospel can be advanced, be still when the chariots will hinder your growth, have no fear of the chariots of this world, and place all your faith in God. Amen.

Sources

Comparative Study Bible. Grand Rapids, Michigan: Zondervan, 1999.

Expository Dictionary of Bible Words. Editor Stephen Renn. Peabody, Massachusetts: Hendrickson Publishers, 2005.

The Harper Collins Bible Dictionary. Editor Paul Achtemeier. New York: Harper Collins, 1996.

The Interlinear NASB-NIV Parallel New Testament in Greek and English. Grand Rapids, Michigan: Zondervan, 1993.